Transcribed
Rhymes

Transcribed
Rhymes

DAVID P. CRESAP

ARPress

ILLUMINATING IDEAS
EMPOWERING VOICES

ARPress
45 Dan Road Suite 5
Canton MA 02021

Hotline:	1(888) 821-0229
Fax:	1(508) 545-7580

Ordering Information:
Quantity sales.Special discounts are available on quantity purchases by corporations, associations, and others.For details, contact the publisher at the address above.

Printed in the United States of America.

ISBN-13:	Paperback	979-8-89330-673-6
	eBook	979-8-89330-672-9

Library of Congress Control Number: 2024902536

Table of Contents

About the Author

I have been writing poetry for better than half a century, and as with many experiences in my life, it began by accident, or to be truthful was it a guided experience, since I truly believe, almost nothing happens by accident.

I have come to this conclusion because of my life's experience. An example is the poem Kindred's Story, in my first book which followed the discovery of these 2 following factual stories in my history.

The back story of this poem is that in about 1840 in Nauvoo Illinois 2 neighbors who were very good friends and associated in many ways and activities in life. Their names were David Eccles and Alonzo Farnsworth. When they left Nauvoo together, David Eccles went to Utah and Alonzo Farnsworth went to Chihuahua, Mexico. In 1975 when the great grandson of David Eccles and the great Granddaughter of Alonzo Farnsworth met and were married on August, 25th. They were together 27 years until she died of an extended illness.

In 1773, an Indian, Chief Logan, of the Mingo tribe in West Virginia, gave a famous speech stating how he enjoyed the white people. He said in his speech, "You never heard of a white man who came to my door that I would not help…. In fact, I would live among the white people were it not for that Monster of Maryland, Colonel Thomas Cresap." 231 years later, Sarah, the direct progeny of Chief Logan, according to Sarah's grandmother, meets David, the direct progeny of Colonel Thomas Cresap.

We were married on April 1 and have been happily married for 18 years. The discovery of this link in linage was an amazing discovery creating the question; could these happenings have been accidental, or could these have been guided?

There are poems that came following thoughts or discussions of religious concepts and ideas, personal experiences and challenges or trials that have affected my attitude. They have shown me wonders that have enhanced my life and understanding.

If we learn to listen, there are energies (spirit guides, ministering angels, The Holy Ghost) or whatever you wish to call them, here on our Earth to help us with the Challenges or Trials we are here to experience and from which and whom, we are to learn. To that end, I have a Grandson, who was diagnosed with "High Functioning Asberger's Disease". As a result, he gets hassled and harassed by family and "friends". I could not understand why because he has skills and talents that are amazing. So. I looked it up to see what is this disease and why should he be hassled.

I discovered, to my amazement that I had 95% of the check marks for "High Functioning Asberger's Disease". But. Medical Science did not have that diagnosis when I was young. I was just a strange kid, but did not get hassled for a label. I admit, I did some very strange things and did get criticized. However, studies have shown that some of our worlds' most advanced scholars, businessmen, and entrepreneurs, have all suffered from this disease. This is because if we get an idea or thought, we delve to the very depth of the subject to figure out the answer as to why it is. This has been one of the greatest blessings in my life, because it gave me the answer as to why I am the way I am, and why my life has gone as it has.

To this end, I have come to understand that our Creator or God knows how to teach me, and is doing so through my life's experiences and the poetry I have been given. My life's work has afforded me a great deal of time to think as I have spent much of it on my own or alone, and as I wondered about life, its meaning, why things are, thoughts will come to me. Often what might follow is a poem which will clarify and sometimes expand the thought. They come in complete form, in about

5 to 15 minutes, then it takes about an hour to decide a title, place them in the organized order, and transcribe them to the computer.

My anthology has become a journal, since they so often follow circumstances in my life and as such, often clarify, and in many cases, ease the stress, pain or anxiety of a situation or just comic relief. They have helped me solidify my purpose, goals, understanding and meaning of our lives here on Earth. The poems come in a universal nature, in that, even though they came to me for a specific reason, they are understood by most people, where in, individuals are able to identify the value, and apply the teaching in the poem to their specific situations

The purpose of this anthology is to allow others to enjoy these poems and to participate in the teachings I have received, which have truly broadened my horizon. Perhaps you might come to the same conclusion as I, in that you will discover, "The more you learn, the more you will realize you don't know", but you will not have to go through the learning process alone without help from another source.

Forward
By Tera L. Cresap Amsbury

A Father. A Papa. A Poet.

The author, born in 1944, has already spent a lifetime experiencing the trials and joys of life. Being in touch with his inner self, he has written and collected a lifetime of poetry. This poetry is dedicated to those who also have a passion for the art and life itself. Hopefully, those who read these poems will feel the passion within the words on these pages. Hopefully also, through the words on these pages, they can experience their souls awaken as well.

The poems are written in a style so they might be understood and enjoyed by the reader in general. In most cases the poems come quickly and some have to be hurriedly written down before they are forgotten. Most of the poems come complete, regarding the trials and experiences of the author, and are as teachings to help give understanding in order to ease the burdens caused by the uncomfortable situations of life's trials.

Loving to play with words, many may start with an idea and a word and are then linked to a rhyming word into the thought of the poem and continued until the thought is completed with all the words needed for the poem being included. These were meant for fun.

Dedication

The poems in this collection
and those I have written are
dedicated to my family.

In most instances
they relate to actual circumstances
and thoughts in my life's journey
and work as a journal
following those experiences
which I have accumulated
throughout
my life.

Acknowledgment

The poems that I have written in this collection
are a result of thoughts, occurrences and
situations that I have experienced.
They come in dreams
and/or strong Spiritual influences
that I am greatly impressed to write down.
They come as lessons to
teach me regarding the foundations of
principals in the teachings of God.

A Flower for Life

A flower blooms
And gives its life.
The life renews
As seeds are cast.
Some fall to grow,
Some feed life's forms.
Its nectar sweet,
Renews in kind,
Even petals, stems,
And leaves provide.
As all rejoice through
Senses guided,
In color, smell, taste
And texture.
Its life, given.

A Leaf

Would I be
A leaf in
The wind?
I would quiver
And fall,
But, I am
A branch.
So I sway
When the wind is
Strong, then
I return to
My place to
Endure the
Seasons
While I grow.

Appearance of Man

A man looks upon a man,
And that is what he sees.
Our Lord will look upon a man
And sees within his heart.

Are we right in what we see,
And thinking what we please?
Should we consider this our view,
Or be it just the start?

Seeing the soul, when we see man,
Acquiring skills as these,
We'll know the value of this view,
Thus add it to our cart.

This influence that comes to us
Might for us, be a tease,
For we don't think our task is real
To mimic Our Lord's part.

So we continue on in life
Accumulating Z's.
Ignoring counsel given us
Be as God and Jesus art.

Being Judge

Judge not lest ye be judged.
Is what our Lord has taught.
We must forgive all other's wrongs
To see what God has wrought.

If we do judge the sins of others
Forgetting they are of our brothers,
Then we might lose our place divine,
That we have thought, "This place is mine."

Know that, there are those who sinned,
Whose trusting choice, has surely thinned,
And so, they erred in acts of life,
Which leads them now in times of strife.

Our goal should be to lift them up,
As one would do with starving pup.
Hate the sin, but not the soul.
This, God has said, must be our role.

To perfect our soul is why we're here.
His teaching is abundant clear.
Be careful with souls begrudged.
"Judge ye not, lest ye be judged."

Christmas Day

Christ was born, but not today.
We celebrate it anyway,
But not with bands and folderol,
Or gifts we buy at local mall.

His gift for us, it had no price,
And blesses us more times than thrice.
It carries us beyond this life,
And cuts through trials as sharpest knife.

As on the hill for us He died,
Unites us all, if it's applied
Within our life to change the heart,
And give to us a brand new start.

So gifts we give should be as such
With value great, beyond a touch.
Through service, lift another's joy
As we are used in His employ.

Participate in Father's plan
To give all joy and show they can
Be carried past this earthly strife
With blessings of Eternal Life.

Consequences

Be careful words that could cause harm
Choose wise your words to help disarm.
Express your love
As One above,
It guides your soul a life of charm.

Be careful all the words you say.
Be they harsh, or simply play.
Once they are said,
They're never dead.
Can affect your lifetime, far away.

Be careful when you criticize.
A tear might come to other's eyes.
Though meant no harm
Could cause alarm
And leave to them a thousand why's.

Be careful thoughts that come to mind.
Strive in your life, bring joy, be kind.
In all you do,
In all be true,
And happiness is what you'll find.

Be careful actions in your life.
Will they bring joy, or cause you strife?
Think before do,
Is best for you,
And march along with drum and fife.

Be careful all the friends you choose.
They'll help you win, or make you lose.

Will they be fair,
Or even care,
Or lead you in a lifelong ruse?

Be careful all the things that come.
Reject a few and embrace some
A shining star
Is how you are.
Make kindness yours, a rule of thumb.

Dreams

Dreams are given for moments of thought,
To guide you in life that your God has wrought.
They detail the trials and challenges given
To focus the ways, in life you are driven.

They're picture of journeys for life's understanding,
To help realize why life was demanding.
Problems are solved and feelings will soften.
The Spirit is there as needed, be often.

So think of your dreams. Apply them with thought.
These treasures are gifts. No price are the bought.
They're yours and they're true, to provide you with guidance,
To help you along, so you sing songs as you dance.

Eternal Joy

For strength in life,
Our trials come.
They are for all, not
Just for some.

It's through
Trust we grow,
To reap the fruits of
What we sow.

Our trust in Him and
Faith we use,
Will bring us joys through
Paths we choose.

To overcome our
Trials so strong,
We need to know what's
Right or wrong.

So trust and learn the
Way to act,
A plan was made for
You, in fact

To gain the blessings
So sublime,
You must endure this
Trialed time,

But, not alone. He's
There for you
To give you strength and
Help you through.

So you can follow
In His plan,
Eternal Joy, aft.
Life of man.

Faith

Faith is our world and ought to be taught,
In deed, in plan, in action and thought.

For all trials in life, from time tiny tot
It carries us through, we shan't be an aught.

It's how things are done and how God has wrought.
The miracles shown, they reveal us His plot.

He's given us blessings, so many he's brought
To keep our life flowing, not stuck as a clot.

He gave us his plan, every tittle and jot,
And told us "Through Faith", we must learn it, or not.

We have to be active, don't stay on the cot.
Think of our progress. Let that be our lot.

Learn at your pace, and learn or be caught,
As stumble in thinking or with worry be fraught.

Work in your mind as if in a slot.
Hold to the rod, keep muscle might taut.

An eye on the prize, that glorious spot,
Keep on and focus, won't go where it's hot.

Not long be our journey by car, plane or yacht,
Yet, this be the journey, the ticket we bought.

When life is a challenge, just give it a swat,
Faith is the answer. It saves the distraught.

Our goal it is righteous, His glory we've sought,
Not worldly goods, neither gold by the pot.

Our life may go smoothly, or tied in a knot,
Our goal be our joy, not the battle we fought.

When trials are upon you, that time on the dot.
Your Faith keeps you happy, and it's your best shot.

Life's not a race, but maybe a trot
So keep it on moving, won't end up a blot.

The end will be lighted by brightest of watt,
When returned to our Father to see what we got.

First, I thought Faith was just belief, but it's not.

Family

It's Family strength that builds together,
For all the time, in all the weather.
You can count on Mom and on Dad
When times are good or times are bad.
The plan is set to progress on,
From times before, to life beyond.
The work is there to help each other,
From Sister down to youngest Brother,
But not just here, there's work to do.
From time beyond, they count on you,
And they will help when you're in need,
By whispers, dreams, their Spirits, heed.
Understand, they are God sent
To help in trials when time is spent.
They count on you. You should on them.
They'll come for you. That's all.
Amen

Father's Day

It's Father's Day,
Hoorah! Hooray!
A card, a gift
Is how you say,
"We love you so,
In every way,
For life and thought,
And what you say
To guide our life,
And not just play."
But, truly on this
Father's Day,
To honor Him
In kind, we may
Take time to kneel,
And to Him, Pray.

For Those Who Wait

Many came to share this world,
But few have shared His Joy.
So plans were made for helping all
For us in His employ.

We need look back to lives long gone,
And help those who were missed
To receive the blessings for them,
So yearning won't persist.

We built a House and searched the past
To fill the gaps unknown.
Thus armed with lists, we understood
To reap those seeds long sown.

The work is hard, long hours spent,
Rewards will come in time,
But, those who wait since journeys past,
Their Joys will be sublime.

Forgiveness

You've been harmed, for they must pay.
It's hard to forgive when
You've been hurt, but, it's God's way.
It's hard to forgive when

A word, an action or something wrong,
Does not beget the kindest song,
So we respond with hardest thought,
And do to those, things we should not.

The teaching is forgive them all,
Be they great, or be they small.
Then we must wait the time until
That God forgives those, whom He will.

If this is done, how great our joy,
As we will gain in His employ.
Blessings grand, now He will send,
To carry us until the end.

It does not stop in earthly race.
It carries forth, Eternal space,
Where we may be Forgiveness Guide
To those dear souls who joined this ride.

God's Way

My Faith has grown over time, and trust,
As God has said, in Him we must
Follow teachings and learn His way
And oft remember to Him, must pray.

He's set a plan and we must listen,
And polish gifts to make them glisten,
So we might help in others' trials,
As we travel our earthly miles.

He's always there to teach the right.
It's up to us to learn to fight
And overcome, endure to end
With garments whitened without a rend.

We're children learning ways so new.
Our Faith and trust guides what to do.
Faith is for us to learn and trust.
It is God's way. Create from dust.

He Needs Me?

What does God need me to be?
Why does He have a need for me?
I'm but one and very small.
What must I know to heed a call?
They say it's written in The Book,
But, how to listen? How to look?
There are so many gone before.
Men of greatness in our lore.
I am but a simple soul.
How could it be to play a role,
In all those lives that I might touch?
What aught I know to be as such
A person, that could change a heart,
To help someone in need, restart
A life misled, to be renewed,
To change a soul from how it's viewed?
Well, I will try to help God's plan,
To bring some joy in life of man,
To uplift him, who's fallen down.
Replace a thorn with Golden Crown.
Then man will live. His joy is found,
And he can help those all around.

Helping Hands

It's that "mutual helping"
That builds us our bond.
It says that "I love you.",
And makes us grow fond.

It tells me, "I need you.",
For now and for ever.
It tells me, "I'm, with you."
As some kind of tether.

So help me when needed,
And even when not.
It gives me the glasses
To see what God wrought.

Don't tell me, "I'm okay.",
That's not in God's plan
To bring us together,
Then be, "also ran".

So, ask me to help you,
And do so, I will,
'Cause then God is watching
From His windowsill.

His Help

The Spirit will come
To visit the soul,
When we are in torment
To make us feel whole.
When challenges visit
And burden us down,
The Spirit comes calling
To bring us around.
It's God's emissary
As someone we knew,
Who returns us the joy,
And helps us work through.
Our trials are a moment,
The blink of an eye,
When all things considered,
As time passes by.
It's but a request,
His Spirit we'll feel.
We only need ask,
And take time to kneel,
Or simply petition
As strife we endure,
His spirit will come,
And comfort ensure.
Don't worry your future.
God has you in plan.
You're one of His children,
And help you He can.

Joy of Passing

Families close and friends so dear
Began a journey that some may fear.
Unknown for us and so we dread,
Depending on the life we've lead.

In truth, it is a time of joy
That God has set for His employ
To bring all back to carry on
A work for all in joyous song.

He helps us pass this awesome door
By those we knew who went before.
No more for them will be their trials,
They're free of pain and burden miles.

So rejoice now, they're in God's hands,
While we stay here in Father's lands.
Tarry not, there's work to do,
And come your time, He'll help you too.

Kindred's Story

History links us all together,
From neighbors, to a kindly feather.
Search your history as it has been
A story linking you and kin.
Before in time, a plan was laid
For future time that Seven made.
It brings joy to hear the story,
Be it kind, or something gory.
Take the time to search your past,
Perhaps to find, a dye was cast,
Or maybe later while in Heaven,
And sanctioned by our number Seven.

Definitions and Story Explanations

Neighbors
Refers to David Eccles (My ancestry) and Alonso Farnsworth (My wife Carole's ancestry) who were very good friends and neighbors in Nauvoo, Illinois circa 1840.

Kindly Feather
Refers to Chief Logan, an Indian chief (My wife Sarah's ancestry), who was very kind and friendly to the white people in the area of West Virginia, circa 1773.

Seven
Refers to God [6 (numerology for evil) plus 1 (numerology for God) equals 7 (Godly/Eternal)]

Gory
Refers to an historical event where Col. Thomas Cresap led a troop of soldiers who reportedly massacred a large number of Chief Logan's family.

Dye was Cast
A plan that perhaps that brought Carole and I, and then later, Sarah and I together.

Life Change

I look around and see my world.
It's like a pot so often swirled.
There was a plan neatly arranged,
As comfort came, it then was changed.
And so anew my world began.
God reset time, another plan?
So now I wait to see the way,
Involved in life as in a play.
The role I have consistently,
Is one as set, but right for me.
It has not changed. Same as before.
It's still a pot to stir some more.

Life's Spirals

Life is circles as forward, it flows.
Like a spiral it moves along time as it goes.
Sometimes up, sometimes down, sometimes joyful or sad,
Depending on trials or lessons we've had.

But we're never alone, as we move on the track,
A Spirit is with us, know,
"It's got your back".
Your lessons in Faith move you forward in trust.
It always will help you. Its reasoning just.

In Heavenly plan we are moving along.
Be joyful while singing the words to your song.
They're different from others.
They're yours. Don't you know.
Like flowers in a garden,
they're the seeds that you sow.

So cultivate wisely, let the circles grow tiny.
A light from Above makes them brighter or shiny.
Go on your way. Don't allow them to fatten.
Make every effort, with God's help, they'll flatten.

We need to have challenge to help us through time.
To grow for our future, that purpose sublime.
No more with the circles, let spirals be gone,
We'll return to the Father, our goal, all along.

Living Memories

Things in memory bring us joy,
A sight, a song, a game, a toy.
A life that's gone is oft renewed
As things of past in mind reviewed.

The smile that comes will soften hearts
As times relived are shared in parts.
It's age that builds those times' abundance
As we relive our lives that were once.

Oh how we worked, lives in the past,
Not thinking how in mind they'd last,
How deep within they might be hidden,
Like bicycles again be ridden.

Live in life, joys to remember
Like laughter, sparks create an ember.
So, eyes that sparkle, return with glee
From times long spent, but still with me.

My Purpose

I came to dwell on Earth below
From Spirit high above.
I came to gain experience
And learn of Father's love.

My goal is growth for Faith beyond
And lead with love and strength,
To return with joy with others all,
Who've learned the breadth and length.

My trials here do make me strong.
This strength for me to share
With those whose trials darken them,
And for them, hard to bear.

So build your love and look afar
For those who need your aid,
And worry not for flaws in you,
For those, the price was paid.

My Time

Time, it says I must comply.
It belongs to me. I don't see why?
It's mine to use as I see fit.
Why must I march in step with it?
I rule my life just as I want.
Time's always there to power flaunt.
My clock is there. Its ticking goes,
On and on and on, who knows?
Will it ever slow or stop?
How many seconds could I lop,
If I don't breathe nor shake my head,
Nor close my eyes, and think instead?
Why does time go and never fail?
It matters most when life is frail,
And I look back o'er shadow cast
Reviewing time as it has passed.
What did I do with all my time?
Just sit and write another rhyme.

Numerology

Every poem I write is nary number six,
For every poem I write, and every word I fix,
In the day, while being bright,
They come to me from in the Light.
They even wake me in the night,
And say to me, that I must write.

The words, they come so clear.
The spirit is so near.
I write them down, fast as I can.
His Spirit touching, guides His plan
To teach the thought that it is for,
And teach that lesson evermore.

I'm but a tool
In Savior's school.
To touch your heart,
To play my part,

For each and every poem I write
That comes in day or in the night,
They're meant for me or meant for you.
It's just my hand that they come through,
To bring you joy, to lift your heart,
So write I must. It is my part.
It's our Lord's work He's given me,
To touch your mind, to set you free.
His kindness comes from up above
On wings of white, a turtle dove.

So on I write again today
The Spirit came with this to say,
"This poem, as all, have come from Heaven.
Thus, this time, it's number Seven."

One Trick Pony

A one trick pony,
Is that my thing   →
To find a bell,
And make it ring?

"Where much is given,
Much is expected."   →
An obscure thought
Is resurrected.

Not just to me,
My aggrandizement,   →
To all must share
For life's enhancement.

So on I teach,
And spread the bounty   →
To each soul,
And every county.

To share my thoughts
That set me free,   →
And hope for all
Their joy will be,

Receive a thought, and
Make it live.
Take it to all
Is how I strive.

These are brought
To me so near.
It is for me
To make them clear.

These precious thoughts
Are brought to me,
Not to keep,
But set them free.

It's not for me
That would be odd.
My journey's long
So on I'll prod.

As great as mine
In later life,
To help them through
This world of strife.

Our Gifts

Gifts we have, some to be found,
For helping those in our surround.
Some for our hands, some for our mind,
Some blend complete, heart, hands in kind.

We're brought to those who need our help,
From aged soul to early whelp.
Then there are those who're brought to us
Who need our help without a fuss.

God gave us gifts and guides our hands,
And touches hearts in distant lands.
Learn your gifts to their perfection.
Apply them oft' with God's correction.

You're known to Him, to help His child.
Understanding how, being meet and mild.
He'll call your name at oddest times
If only to transcribe His rhymes.

Pain

I have pain, but why? Who knows?
Not always there, it comes and goes.
With x-rays taken, the doctor said,
"There's nothing there. It's in your head."
How can that be? I feel it now.
It's in my head? That's wrong some how.
I'll take a nap, maybe a pill.
It seems so strange, I don't feel ill.
In my thoughts, I don't know whether
It is my head, or just the weather.
Perhaps I'll try an herb or lotion,
Or maybe some exotic potion.
In all this world must be an answer,
Not just the same old "song and dancer."
I guess I'll try for something new,
Put my foot in another shoe.
I've heard there's other things that work.
Techniques around. I should not shirk.
An open mind is what it takes.
I'll take a chance, for Heaven sakes.
Then that's If what I try will make it go,
For me, my row to hoe.
I'll use this knowledge, apply my trust,
Change my life, might be a must.
The facts are there, answers abound.
The PAIN IS GONE. The peace I've found.
There is much more, so I will go,
And study long. There's more to know.
Trust in God to make things clear,
And know through Faith, the answer's near.
It's not just man who knows the cure.
It's been on earth quite long and pure.
We must apply our thoughts and vision.
Use our minds not some incision.
The answer's there for us to find,
For God is sweet. His wisdom kind.

Pennies

Since pennies last
A memory,
They must be saved.
So much alike
They are.
They mount up,
Tarnished or shiny.
One is little, but
Many is a life.
Save them all
For the day alone
And count them out,
But, keep them quiet
Lest someone steal
Them all away.

Perfection

Perfection is the goal for man.
Become Supreme, not also ran.
We take a step and learn a little,
Not all at once, but jot and tittle.

A plan, we asked, "Please let us try?"
Yet, now we wonder and question why?
We play and err and make a fuss.
Did we forget the goal for us?

The goal was set before we came
To strive and trust in Father's name.
Through Faith we'll learn, so take the time,
Eventually we'll make it rhyme.

Through Faith is how you'll make it fun
As questions come, each, one by one.
An answer to this earthly quiz?
"Be ye therefore perfect, as Father is."

Our journey's short, just blink your eye
To know the time that we must try.
Think back in life, a year was long,
And now they pass like words in song.

Our Father watches and guides our path.
He helps us learn avoiding wrath.
So step by step we'll reach our goal
To learn the value of our soul.

Prelude to an Answered Prayer II

Another rhyme will come in time,
As needed for its teaching.
Sing the song and toll the chime,
Its value is not preaching.

The feelings come as mellow hum,
But never brassy screeching,
Or lots of sound to drowned them out
With many words of speeching.

If need is there, no gaps are left
They're filled with Spirit breaching.
To touch your heart, throughout your soul
Your garment's pure from bleaching.

Not just for one, but all you've done,
The cleansing is far reaching.
This thought is clear to bring us near,
A Royal Throne beseeching.

Prophet's Counsel

The Prophet's teachings are for all,
Involving all our life.
If we should heed this counsel true,
It can diminish strife.

From birth to death and life beyond
It expands our earthly view.
It opens doors and thoughts to all,
And not just what we knew.

His words be revelations pure
To guide us from on High,
To answer questions from our toils,
To explain the reasons why.

So listen with your hearts as well,
Not just your ears for sound,
'Cause learning comes to help us live
Beyond what We have found.

Questions?

Do you wonder or question why,
What made the Earth or made the sky,
Or how it is, I came to be,
Or other people that I see?
Have you thought, "Where will I go?
When life is through?" I just don't know.
These questions bounced around my head.
What's going to happen when I'm dead?
Is this the end? There is no more?
What is beyond, for me in store?

For me the answers all have come,
And eased my mind so straight and plumb,
That I don't worry or question why,
My inner me did satisfy.
Now I know that if I wonder,
The answer comes as loud as thunder,
Or maybe just a quiet thought
To teach me that, what God has wrought.

My knowledge grows from many sources.
It fills my being. Like blood it courses,
And touches every "being" part
From mind and soul, it fills my heart.

So it can do the same for you,
If you are willing to listen to,
A sound, a thought that starts you off
Then leads you to a bounty trough,
Where you'll be filled and even sated
With thoughts and knowledge highly rated.
Just know this bounty's from on High,

To answer all your questions why,
And give you peace for you to know,
As all along in life you go.

There will be more as need arises,
Not just for you, He emphasizes.
You must share this help with all,
Be they great or be they small,
So they will know the answer's there,
If they desire or even care.
In matters that concern their life,
So they can march with drum and fife.

This knowledge for us, is a gift
To give us strength and give us lift.
It is a gift to very few,
But now this gift was meant for you.

Quiet Impressions

If you're impressed,
It is the best
To listen to the voices.
They are there
To help you where
You have so many choices.

A Spirit comes that knows your life
And guides you through the miles,
To help you through the times of worry,
Of your burdens and your trials.

So get to know those voices clear,
That come from up above.
They come to you when you're in fear,
Surrounding you with love.

Those thoughts will come from
Somewhere deep impressing actions true
If you will listen, act with your soul
You'll know this trust for you.

It may be hard when you begin
To hear those subtle hints,
But in due time, the goal within,
Experience, convince.

Revelation

A thought, a feeling,
An energy flow,
A revelation for you
To enhance what you know.

Perhaps it's a question
That's set in your mind,
Brought through to your spirit
To guide you in kind.

Its frequency touching
To match what you say
It's a sound in vibration
Linking your D.N.A.

He knows through your spirit
Exactly what's needed.
A teaching, a guiding,
The thought must be heeded.

He'll never mislead you, and,
Your eyes? They will glisten.
It's just up to you,
If you're willing to listen.

Spirit Care

When you feel you're all alone,
Realize you're not.
There's always life within your realm,
Unless you block with thought.

A Spirit force looks after you
To guide you in your life.
It's up to you to understand
And sense, a feeling rife.

A hope is there from Guide beyond
To share the Joy with you,
So you can feel and build the Joy
With those of wanting, too.

An energy is in your life
That spreads to those around
And brings to them a silent sense
Of that Joy you've found.

Block not your soul, and feel your guide.
The energy do share,
So you will grow beyond this realm
And feel the Spirit care.

Teachings in Poetry

A vignette of my life,
They come like drum and fife.
For me to understand,
For me, there is a plan.
I am to worry not.
This plan, it was God wrought.
The same it is for you.
This plan, He's put you through,
And helping you along,
This life and worldly throng.
Your joy will be sublime,
And will not end with time.
For on and on it goes,
Without end? Who knows?
The blessings' there for you,
Could be for all. Who knew?

Thanks Giving Day

Thanks Giving Day again is near,
Though blessings flow throughout the year.
Since Blessings come on every day by day,
Should we not take time to pray,
And thank our Father for our joy,
For food we eat, and our employ,
And simple things? Those things we see
That lift our hearts, and bring us glee?
Each breath we take, and sound we hear,
Each thought we have to make things clear?
And so, we should take time to pray,
To make each hour, Thanks Giving Day,
And not just make it once a year
To show our God, we need Him here.
or Thankfulness, that state of mind,
Brings joy and blessings to our kind.

The Bus Ride

Life is a window
On a bus ride
To open to darken
Or change the inside.

Rain can be outside
Or allowed to come in.
Sights to be seen
Can bring on a grin.

The sun can be bright,
Even warm or quite hot,
Or covered by clouds
Bringing darkness or not.

For sure it is changing
As pictures glide by,
It's a taste and a wonder.
Just give it a try.

The Gift of a Child

We're given gifts from our Dear Lord.
They're called children, and they're our ward,
To teach and guide, then how to win,
Especially how to keep from sin.
Their minds are new from spirit land
For us to show what Father planned,
To bring them back for joys unbound
With knowledge true, that they have found.
They start with bodies small and cute,
And learn from us. This question moot.
They come with spirits pure and bold,
And embrace teachings they are told.
 It up to us to be prepared,
And pass along what God has shared.
To guide us as we heard the voice
That helps us as we make our choice.
In righteousness we lead our lives,
While watching as our child strives
To adapt this spirit to our world
In spotless white not slightly merled.
Their choice to come brought them such joy.
Be they girl or be they boy.
Many knew the life selected,
And through it all would be connected
To the family right for them,
And so they came with joy,
Amen.

The Gifts of God

God gives us gifts
For helping others,
Be they unknown,
Or of our brothers.

Please do not worry
About a payment,
Cause He is there
For every raiment.

Your needs are met,
And even more,
Just help and see
For you in store.

So, use your gifts
In every county,
And watch and see,
No end to bounty.

The more you give
To help His child
With attitude
Being kind and mild,

There is no worry
For your life,
So march along
With drum and fife.

You will receive
If you should heed,
And use His gifts
For other's need.

The Most Precious Gift

The Holy Ghost
Of the Godhead sure
Is here to help
Whose souls are pure.

He'll guide and help
In times of strife,
Especially you,
Throughout your life.

He'll answer questions,
Touch your heart.
He'll bring you joy.
Just do your part.

He is your gift and
Yours to trust.
His answers true,
His reasoning's Just.

He's kind with love
And patient too.
He is the Gift
That's best for you.

So, honor keep
In all you do.
He'll be your guide.
He's here for you.

The Power of Faith

"Faith is a power, not just a belief."
It was used for Creation, not simply relief.
We need to have learning for use in our day
To build understanding and know it's God's way.

Faith is the power that helps us to know
And guides us in life where miracles show.
It's not just for now, to give us the strength
To broaden our world in its breadth and its length.

Faith must be learned to live in our future,
A valuable part empowering our culture.
It's for now and forever, Eternal repose,
To train us in all, to live what God knows.

The Student

"When the student is ready,
The teacher will come."
Many words, they are taught.
Who receives? Only some.

Through parables spoken,
The values are hidden.
To unrighteous ears,
Their meaning forbidden.

To ears that can hear them.
These teachings are precious.
They're spoken for all
In our hearts, they do touch us.

With meaning so pure,
And clarity strong,
Thus each time we use them
We'll never go wrong.

So open your heart,
In your mind let them come.
You may be the many,
But, could be the some.

The Warning

What has happened
In my life?
How could I be
In such a strife?
The Spirit always
Gives me warning,
So I am ready
In the morning.
How could this
Happen such to me?
Did I neglect
To listen?

Thoughts in Time

My time is spent in wondrous thought.
As ever now should I, or not,
Participate in life as real,
Or jump around in touch and feel?
If I should choose the latter more,
What would the path for me in store?
The charm it be, for changing wind
Might in my being cause me to rend.
So, maybe I should stay my path
To feel a joy instead of wrath.

Toil of Life

Life can truly, really suck,
If you let your mind dwell in the muck.
You plan and plan and plan to gain,
And on that day, it starts to rain.

You try and work and try again.
You push your life and pray, amen.
So long you wait for time to pass,
Enduring life, and beings crass.

You hope and plead for shining ray,
That Spirit gift of brighter day.
Just worry not. Your thoughts, renew.
For God will bring what's right for you.

So strive you must, be strong in might.
Direct your work to other's plight.
Forget your own, in life you strive.
The gift of God, makes you alive.

When Snakes Appear

When snakes appear along a path,
In dreams of yours, just do the math,
And "Count your blessings one by one,
To see the wonders God has done."

Understand, He is your guide,
But walks with your step, side by side,
To see that you are filled with joy
For use and trust in His employ.

Those snakes are there to give us pause,
And think of why. What is the cause?
It helps us grow and makes us free
To live a life that we might see

How blessed we are every day
That Father helps us on our way,
And blocks those snakes that could strike us,
So carry on and do not cuss.

For He is here and with you now,
To help you live with glee somehow,
And share with those whom you have found,
Who've struggled 'til you came around.

Window or Door?

Dreams are a window
God lets you see through
To guide you in life,
And in challenges too.

It's up to your thinking to
Figure it them out,
No kicking, nor screaming
Not even a pout.

They're often quite simple
And usually pure,
But sometimes they're different,
And seem quite obscure.

At times they're a story
To encourage your thought,
At times it's a picture
To see your life's plot.

So think of that window,
And what it is for,
Just figure it out
It might be a door.

Wondrous Life

Wondrous things, in my life are coming.
Should I just sit and continue humming,
Or should I sit and plan ahead,
Not simply wait until I'm dead?
My thoughts continue as I go,
But wonder still just where to go.
Do I tell others of thoughts that come?
Be still for all, but just tell some?
The thoughts are clear and I do know,
The plan for me, as I should go,
But others have not lived my world,
And so their thoughts? My mind is twirled.
I feel so guided in my plan.
I have to trust. Do as I can.
For others? Let them be as may.
Consider some of what they say.
Stay quiet as I move along.
Continue listening to the song
That plays so loudly in my ear,
And know that others, just can't hear.
My history's guided, to this, my time,
And helped me learn through words that rhyme.
So on, I'll go in helping others,
And knowing that, they are my brothers.
Stay in tune for path to follow,
So not get stuck in muddy wallow.
For as I go, I will succeed.
If guided listening, I do heed.

Words of Warmth

Words of Warmth", that we should speak,
These words of warmth are what I seek.
These are the words we've heard before.
These are the words we daren't ignore.

They're meaning? Gifts – value sublime
That come to us in quiet time.
They're in your mind, in your heart, you feel,
But mostly heard when times you kneel.

These words of warmth are from above
To grant us power, unbounded love,
Which we should use to help for all
Lest they don't hear to heed the call.

So look for them in times of need.
Follow them, their meanings heed.
Their timing's right. Their meaning's true,
But best of all, they're meant for you.

Youth's Wisdom

The wisdom of youth
Is oft-times hidden
In an impulse.

Each impulse
Gives birth to
A spontaneous
Burst of joy.

This joy they share
With those who live
In memories,

And in turn,
Their wisdom grows
To again hide behind
The impulse of youth.

Carole -
Grandmother
Mother and Wife
Collection

For Carole
From Dee

Though souls depart
As time has gone,
Our love does not,
For it lives on.

A mission done
This journey's end,
New life begins.
No clothes we rend.

T'is sad this day
We bid adieu,
And wait for time
To start anew.

We traveled far
And trials found.
We learned a lot.
Let joys abound!

Our family grew
And will expand
With life apart,
Which was not planned.

You'll touch us now
And we will feel,
For you'll be here;
We know your zeal.

=>

Our hearts remember
Your counsel sweet;
Your expectation
We'll surely meet.

And with each child
You teach with pride,
We'll bring with love
And honor guide.

And when time comes
For us rejoin,
I'll greet you tender,
Kisses purloin.

Then on we'll go
No more apart,
For eternal life,
This just the start.

So comfort now
To all who mourn,
We will move on
Our sins are shorn.

Christ paid the debt.
We will be free
To match His love
Eternally.

^

"I'm Different Now."

"I'm different now."
Rings in my ear.
(I'm happy now.)
T'is that I hear?   >

"I'm different now."
T'is that her plea,
To tell me how
She waits for me?

"I'm different now."
It calls to me
To tell me how
From me she's free?   >

"I'm different now."
Is that her clue?
Saying to me,
"I want for you?"

"I'm different now."
Can mean both things.
So in my head
This torment rings.   >

"I'm different now."
I wish were clear.
It torments me,
My heart does sear.

"I'm different now."
I can't forget,
And how it came
From you, my pet.   >

"I'm different now."
Please let me see,
The meaning true
With clarity.

"I'm different now."
I will not rest.
Until for sure
I know what's best.   >

"I'm different now."
My heart will rend.
Until I die
Not know the end.

Mourning

Your passing causes me to mourn.
' Miss you with every breath.
I miss you more with every day.
I even think of death.
I will never follow through, but
Still my heart is breaking.
Each night I sleep for just an hour,
Your memory keeps me waking.
I close my eyes and see your face
In life or in your struggle.
I want to have you in my arms,
Your sweet embrace and snuggle.

The loneliness I feel for now,
I'm told will pass through sorrow.
I have to wait, no joy will come,
Perhaps it will tomorrow.
Each soul is different, I know.
I wish that mine be steady,
But I still grieve. 'will mourn for you',
Until my heart be ready.
I know not when that time will come,
And I cannot prepare.
I only know It comes in time,
When Spirit leads me there.

And so for now, I'll work and wait,
My spirit please be strong.
Be patient, not aloof my soul
Let not my heart be wrong.

My Dove – Carole

Carole you are my love,
My white and soaring dove
Up high so you may see,
And watching over me.
My true and beating heart
Who, for me did start
Our growing family.
Until you then were free
From pain and worried mind,
Not thinking me unkind.
To me you were so dear,
But now I'm left with fear,
To search both far and wide
For one you bring with pride,
To help me journey on.
This life to do no wrong,
That to you I return
With all that I did learn.

My Trial

Is it so wrong, my missing you?
They say that I should mourn.
I need to have you by my side.
I can't, and feel forlorn.

I long to feel your presence near.
A warmth and smile embrace,
Should I search for one so soon,
Who'd ably take your place?

You knew before you became free
From this trial so hard,
That I would long for someone near
And could not draw your card.

I fear for time has not gone long
And every day I cry
To feel a spirit close to mine,
Yet protocol deny.

So search I must while I'm alone
And keep my thoughts to me,
For when its right, and I will know,
Your spirit set me free.

To choose the one who you'll approve,
Your help I'm counting on.
For you will know her spirit true
Let loneliness be gone!

The Departure

A tear is how she said goodbye,
Now quiet peaceful sleep.
Her family round her softly cry,
Her spirit does not weep.

How mournful all her children sigh
How slowly does time creep.
We all do wish her spirit fly,
While ours are in a heap.

Her toil begun in heaven's sky
In Christ's work does she reap.
Her spirit stays in our mind's eye,
And in our hearts we keep.

We will be strong and always try
In effort will we leap.
We never will forget and why?
In us, her blood does seep.

The Dream

My love she swims amid a pool
And comes upon a fruit.
She savors it and then swims on
While thinking of its root.

The water soiled yet she swims on,
Again a morsel found.
She eats its sweet and tasty flesh
And searches all around.

She desires to depart the pool,
But told she cannot yet
For she must linger still a while,
Her journey time is set.

Now on she goes seeking relief,
A desire to be clean,
She spies another fruit more choice
The want for it is keen.

She takes its lush abundant meat
And swims still far and wide,
Until a voice does call to her,
She may now come inside.

So now she swims up to the edge.
She thankfully climbs out.
She cleans herself with water pure,
And then begins to shout.

"My mission done, it is complete."
The journey surely through,
"Now I will wait for you to come,
My love, forever, you."

The Gift

A most wonderful thing
Has happened to me.
I've been given a gift
That's setting me free,

From anguish and woe
And worry and strife,
And how should I feel?
It came from my wife,

Who loved me so dearly
And knows of my heart,
As soon as she left
My loneliness start.

She searched far and wide
To bring me such joy,
And touched deep inside me
Her kindness employ.

It started so small
And grew with such force,
There was no denying
This path is my course.

I've come from such darkness
And heartache inside,
To serenity's calm,
It can't be denied

This gift, it was chosen
From many, it's true,
And now she has shown me,
I'm your gift to you.

How truly she loved me
And this I do know
My joy, it is growing
I've someone to show.

Our life's journey forward
Is touched through the veil
And angels are watching
As through storms we sail.

For now and forever
This feeling is thus,
This gift that was given,
Was given to us.

Now we'll share our trials.
Our joys, they us lift.
We must always remember,
That we were a gift.

www.ingramcontent.com/pod-product-compliance
Lightning Source LLC
Chambersburg PA
CBHW020333130626
46549CB00003B/1150